ALBUM OF DINOSAURS

THERE WERE DINOSAURS with bodies as big as a railroad boxcar and dinosaurs no bigger than a present-day chicken. There were dinosaurs with webbed feet and bills like ducks . . . dinosaurs with 2-ounce brains in 2-ton bodies . . . dinosaurs with an extra "brain" at the base of their spines. There were dinosaurs with nostrils on top of their heads . . . dinosaurs with huge sail-like fins on their backs . . . and dinosaurs with horns on their faces, on their heads, on their tails, on their "thumbs." And they all lived between 200 million and 70 million years ago, during the Age of Reptiles.

Tom McGowen writes accurately and vividly of these amazing beasts, re-creating a world in which herds of triceratopsians grazed, in which Allosaurus tracked and attacked Apatosaurus, in which the great female Protoceratops dropped her eggs in a nest that would be unearthed tens of millions of years later by searching scientists. And artist Rod Ruth gives exciting form to the animals in a series of carefully researched full-color and black-and-white illustrations.

Altogether, more than 40 dinosaurs are included here, along with other creatures of the period. There are an introductory section on dinosaurs in general, an index to aid in locating the creature of one's choice, and a welcome pronunciation guide to assist with tongue-twisting names. ALBUM OF DINOSAURS, in which text and illustrations enhance each other, is another in the lengthening list of Rand McNally ALBUMS.

Album of Dinosaurs

By TOM McGOWEN
Illustrated by ROD RUTH

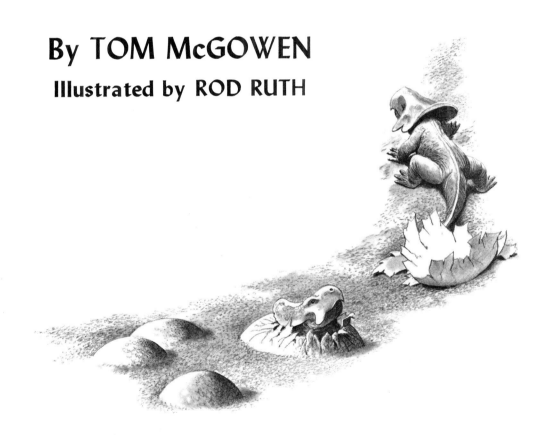

RAND McNALLY & COMPANY

Chicago • New York • San Francisco

Illustrations prepared under the direction of
Dr. Rainer Zangerl
Chairman, Department of Geology
Field Museum of Natural History
Chicago, Illinois

Text reviewed and authenticated by
Dr. Dale Russell
Chief, Palaeontology Division
National Museum of Natural Sciences
Ottawa, Ontario, Canada

First printing, 1972
Second printing, 1973
Third printing, 1974
Fourth printing, March, 1975
Fifth printing, October, 1975
Sixth printing, August, 1976

Library of Congress Cataloging in Publication Data
McGowen, Tom.
    Album of dinosaurs.
    SUMMARY: A brief introduction to the history and char-
acteristics of dinosaurs in general and specific descriptions of
twelve different kinds.
    1. Dinosaurs—Juvenile literature.   [1. Dinosaurs]
I. Ruth, Rod, illus.   II. Title.
QE862.D5M28   568'.19   74-188730
ISBN 0-528-82024-9
ISBN 0-528-80152-X (lib. bdg.)

Portion of "The Dinosaur" by Bert L. Taylor,
page 18, reprinted courtesy of the *Chicago Tribune*

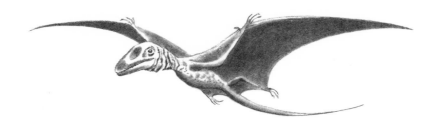

Contents

Dinosaurs — THE TERRIBLE LIZARDS

IN A THICK tangle of forest on the edge of a small lake, an oddly shaped, rather clumsy-looking animal shuffles about in search of food. It has a large, bulky body, a long, thick tail, and a surprisingly small head on the end of a long neck.

As the animal moves about through the foliage, it walks upright on its two, stout back legs, holding its smaller front legs in front of its chest, like arms. Its feet are five-toed, with blunt claws on the toes; its forefeet are much like hands, with four fingers and a large thumb.

When the creature spies a clump of leafy plants growing close to the ground, it drops to all fours and begins munching leaves with its blunt teeth. From nose to tip of tail this plant-eating animal is 20 feet long —about twice as long as an African elephant.

Suddenly, another animal emerges from the forest. It, too, walks upright, but its neck is much shorter and its head much bigger than the plant eater's. Its mouth bristles with sharp teeth.

With a single bound this animal hurls itself upon the plant eater, sinking its teeth into the other's neck. The plant eater strug-

8

BRACHIOSAURUS

Rhamphorhynchus

gles but is quickly subdued. The sharp-toothed creature begins to rip chunks of flesh from the quivering body.

These two creatures were dinosaurs—Plateosaurus, a plant eater, and Teratosaurus, a flesh eater. They lived in Europe about 180 million years ago, and they were just two of the many kinds of strange creatures that hunted and fought and roamed everywhere in the world during the time that is called the Age of Reptiles. Dinosaurs were kings of the world then, as common as people are now. There were dinosaurs with horns, dinosaurs with arm-

ALLOSAURUS

Plateosaurus

ored bodies, and dinosaurs with duckbills. There were dinosaurs that were the biggest land animals that have ever lived and dinosaurs that were no bigger than chickens.

Just what were these strange animals? The name *dinosaur* means "terrible lizard." But dinosaurs were not lizards. And only the big flesh-eating dinosaurs could really be called "terrible." Most kinds of dinosaurs were plant eaters and were really no more terrible than the giraffe or buffalo or other wild animal of today.

The dinosaurs were, of course, reptiles. This means they belong to the same scaly-skinned, cold-blooded family as lizards, snakes, alligators, crocodiles, and turtles. But dinosaurs were quite different from all these other reptiles. There is nothing like a dinosaur living in the world today.

What made the dinosaurs different from other reptiles? It wasn't size, because although many dinosaurs were giants, some of them were no bigger than many lizards, snakes, and crocodiles living now. And it wasn't their strange appearance, because many of today's reptiles are every bit as odd-looking as any of the dinosaurs were.

The main thing that made dinosaurs so different from today's living reptiles is the way their bodies were constructed. Nearly every reptile now living, except for snakes and legless lizards, walks on four legs that sprawl out from the sides of its body. But the first kinds of dinosaurs were all *two-legged* animals that walked and ran on their back legs (as we do) and used their smaller front legs like arms. Even the four-

legged dinosaurs were really just two-legged animals that walked on all fours because their bodies were too big and bulky for only two legs to carry.

Of course, it took many millions of years for two-legged dinosaurs to turn into four-legged ones. And that's an important fact to remember about dinosaurs—they didn't all live at the same time. There were dinosaurs living in this world for 130 million years, and many kinds of dinosaurs lived millions of years apart from each other. In fact, some of the dinosaurs we know about were *ancestors* of some of the other dinosaurs!

Nearly everything we know about dinosaurs has been learned from fossils. Fossils are records of plant and animal life that have been preserved in stone. For example, dinosaurs walked in mud and left footprints, and the mud hardened into stone with the footprints still in it. From such prints scientists can tell how dinosaurs walked and ran. Many dinosaur bones and skeletons that turned to stone over millions of years have been found. From them, scientists can tell how big a dinosaur was, how much it weighed, what it ate, and sometimes even how well it could see, hear, and smell. Prints of dinosaur skin and even petrified "mummies" of dinosaurs have been found, telling us much about what dinosaurs looked like. Even petrified dinosaur eggs have been found, solving the mystery of how dinosaur babies were born.

New fossils and new ways of learning things from fossils are being found all the time, adding to our knowledge of dino-

Snake

Turtle

Tortoise

Lizard

Present-day Reptiles

Alligator

Crocodile

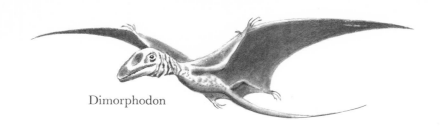

Dimorphodon

saurs. Sometimes these discoveries show us that what we had thought to be true about certain dinosaurs is all wrong. Sometimes dinosaurs even have to be renamed—which is why, if you've read about dinosaurs before, you may be surprised to find some old friends with new names in this book.

Remember, then, that dinosaurs were reptiles—but not like any reptiles that are living today—and that they didn't all live at the same time. Here's a list that will help you understand just when each kind of prehistoric animal you'll read about in this book was alive.

200 MILLION TO 180 MILLION YEARS AGO

Coelophysis	(see-loh-FY-ses)
Plateosaurus	(PLAD-ee-uh-SAW-ruhs)
Proganochelys	(proh-GAN-oh-CHEL-eez)
Teratosaurus	(ter-AT-uh-SAW-ruhs)
Trilophosaurus	(try-LOH-fuh-SAW-ruhs)

180 MILLION TO 160 MILLION YEARS AGO

Megalosaurus	(MEG-uh-loh-SAW-ruhs)
Scelidosaurus	(SEL-uh-doh-SAW-ruhs)

160 MILLION TO 135 MILLION YEARS AGO

Allosaurus	(AL-uh-SAW-ruhs)
Apatosaurus	(uh-PAT-uh-SAW-ruhs)
Archaeopteryx	(AHR-kee-AHP-tuh-riks)
Brachiosaurus	(BRAK-ee-oh-SAW-ruhs)
Camarasaurus	(KAM-uh-ruh-SAW-ruhs)
Camptosaurus	(KAMP-tuh-SAW-ruhs)
Ceratosaurus	(seh-RAT-uh-SAW-ruhs)
Chialingosaurus	(chy-uh-LING-uh-SAW-ruhs)
Compsognathus	(kahmp-SAHG-nuh-thuhs)
Dapedius	(duh-PEE-dee-uhs)
Dimorphodon	(dy-MOHR-foh-dahn)
Diplodocus	(dih-ploh-DAHK-uhs)

Kentrosaurus	(KENT-ruh-SAW-ruhs)
Omosaurus	(OH-muh-SAW-ruhs)
Ornitholestes	(awr-NITH-uh-LEH-steez)
Rhamphorhynchus	(RAM-fuh-RING-kuhs)
Stegosaurus	(STEG-uh-SAW-ruhs)
Theriosuchus	(thehr-ee-oh-SOO-kuhs)

135 MILLION TO 100 MILLION YEARS AGO

Acanthopholis	(ah-KAN-thuh-FOHL-is)
Hypsilophodon	(HIP-suh-LAHF-uh-dahn)
Iguanodon	(eh-GWAHN-uh-dahn)
Polacanthus	(POHL-uh-KAN-thuhs)
Pterodactylus	(TERR-uh-DAK-teh-luhs)

100 MILLION TO 70 MILLION YEARS AGO

Albertosaurus	(al-BER-tuh-SAW-ruhs)
Anatosaurus	(uh-NAT-uh-SAW-ruhs)
Ankylosaurus	(ANG-kih-loh-SAW-ruhs)
Chasmosaurus	(CHAS-muh-SAW-ruhs)
Corythosaurus	(kuh-RITH-uh-SAW-ruhs)
Euoplocephalus	(yoo-uh-pluh-SEF-uh-luhs)
Hesperornis	(HES-puh-RAWR-nehs)
Kritosaurus	(KRY-tuh-SAW-ruhs)
Lambeosaurus	(LAM-bee-uh-SAW-ruhs)
Monoclonius	(MAHN-uh-KLOH-nee-uhs)
Nodosaurus	(NOHD-uh-SAW-ruhs)
Ornithomimus	(awr-NITH-uh-MY-muhs)
Pachycephalosaurus	(PAK-ee-SEF-al-uh-SAW-ruhs)
Pachyophis	(pak-ee-OH-fuhs)
Paleoscincus	(PAE-lee-uh-SKINK-us)
Parasaurolophus	(par-uh-sawr-AHL-uh-fuhs)
Pentaceratops	(PEN-tuh-SERR-uh-tahps)
Phobosuchus	(foh-boh-SOOK-uhs)
Pinacosaurus	(pyn-AK-uh-SAW-ruhs)
Protoceratops	(PROH-doh-SERR-uh-tahps)
Pteranodon	(tuh-RAN-uh-dahn)
Spinosaurus	(SPYN-uh-SAW-ruhs)
Struthiomimus	(STROO-thee-oh-MY-muhs)
Styracosaurus	(sty-RAK-uh-SAW-ruhs)
Titanosaurus	(ty-TAN-uh-SAW-ruhs)
Torosaurus	(TOH-roh-SAW-ruhs)
Triceratops	(try-SERR-uh-tahps)
Tyrannosaurus	(teh-RAN-uh-SAW-ruhs)

Tyrannosaurus Rex

Triceratops

Coelophysis—ONE OF THE FIRST

THE WAVES of a great green sea surged and swelled and came rolling in with a hiss upon a red, sandy shore. The land stretched away from the shore, low and flat, crossed by many lazily flowing rivers and dotted with shallow lakes. No grass or flowers covered the red soil, but there were clumps of ferns everywhere, and the river-banks were choked with thick clusters of 15-foot-high rushes.

The land rose gradually, and on the high ground dense forests sprawled. Trees with lacy clusters of fan-shaped leaves grew in the forests, together with stubby, treelike plants that had trunks shaped like balls and barrels, crowned with circles of feathery leaves. Farther inland on the higher ground the black, pointed snouts of volcanoes poked up at the sky. From time to time one of them might rumble sullenly and spout spumes of black smoke into the air. And sometimes one of them would explode into fiery fury, and for days the sun would be blotted out by dark, drifting clouds of ash.

This was the western part of the North American continent—180 million years ago.

A great many kinds of animals crept and crawled and skittered and slogged about on the red flatlands and in the forests. In the wet places there were short-tailed, four-footed creatures that looked somewhat like lizards but were really amphibians. Dragonflies were numerous, and roaches and spiders swarmed everywhere, looking much the same as they do today and doing much the same sorts of things they do now. There were no ants, bees, or butterflies though, nor would there be for many millions of years. And there were no birds. But there were tiny, furry, ratlike creatures that darted and dashed about in the under-brush. They were ancestors of the mammals.

And there were plenty of cold-blooded, scaly-skinned reptiles. In fact, there were so many reptiles in the world that scientists call this period the Age of Reptiles—an age that lasted 130 million years!

Many of those reptiles of long ago resembled some of the kinds of reptiles that are living now. There were turtles, much like the turtles of today except that those ancient turtles couldn't pull their heads and legs all the way into their shells. There were lots of lizards. And there were small beasts that looked like snub-nosed croco-

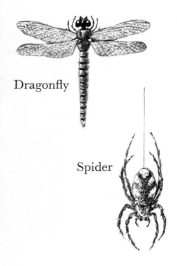

Dragonfly

Spider

Proganochelys

COELOPHYSIS

Trilophosaurus

Williamsonia

diles, and large beasts that looked like long-nosed crocodiles.

But there was one kind of creature that looked like nothing else alive, then or now. For, while all the other reptiles moved clumsily about on all fours, this animal walked and ran upright on its two, birdlike back legs. It ran swiftly, with its body bent forward and its long neck and tail stretched stiffly out. Its head bobbed up and down as it ran, and it held its arms close to its chest.

This animal was something brand new in the world of 180 million years ago, and there's nothing at all like it in the world now. For this two-legged, running reptile was one of the first of those strange creatures, the dinosaurs.

Scientists have named this early dinosaur Coelophysis, and they know quite a lot about it from some marvelously well-preserved fossil skeletons found in New Mexico. Even though Coelophysis was a dinosaur and the word *dinosaur* means "terrible lizard," Coelophysis probably wouldn't seem very terrible if you saw it running about in a zoo. We think of dinosaurs as being huge. But Coelophysis, like most of the first kinds of dinosaurs, was rather small. It was only about 8 feet long, and nearly half of that length was tail. It was about 3 feet tall standing upright, and no more than 2 feet tall when it ran because of the way it bent its body forward. It was slender and birdlike, with hollow bones like the bones of a bird. *Coelophysis* means "hollow form," referring to these bones. It weighed only 40 or 50 pounds—not much more than an average eight-year-old child.

But while Coelophysis might not seem very terrible to you, it probably caused real terror to the many kinds of small reptiles that lived with it on the red New Mexico flatlands those many millions of years ago. For Coelophysis was a flesh eater, and the flesh it ate was torn in chunks from the bodies of animals it hunted and caught. It probably ate any small animal that wasn't fast enough to get away or well armored enough to be safe from its sharp, little teeth. There's even some evidence that Coelophysis was a cannibal and sometimes feasted on young animals of its own kind, as many snakes, crocodiles, and other reptiles do today.

We can tell that Coelophysis was a flesh eater by looking at the teeth in its fossil skull. Those teeth are small, but they're sharp as daggers, and they have saw-toothed edges like the cutting edge of a steak knife. Coelophysis's front legs also show that it was a flesh eater. They are little arms with four-fingered hands, and on three of the fingers are sharp claws. Coelophysis could close its hands, which means that it probably used them for grabbing things. It may have held its prey with those little clawed hands while the knifelike teeth did their job of cutting the animal to pieces. If you've ever seen a picture of an eagle or owl or other bird of prey holding a rat or rabbit in its claws as it tears into the flesh with its beak, you can easily imagine how Coelophysis must have looked as it was having dinner.

Coelophysis's back legs were completely different from the front ones. They were

14

Cycad

almost exactly like the legs of a bird. The feet had three toes with sharp claws on them, much like the feet of many modern birds. Footprints of three-toed dinosaurs have been found in many parts of the world. They were made when dinosaurs trudged or trotted through thick mud that hardened into rock over many millions of years. Some of these footprints are just about the size of Coelophysis's feet and may have been made by some of these active, little dinosaurs. Mixed in with the footprints is an occasional print of a dinosaur's bottom, which seems to show that when Coelophysis got tired it probably sat down to rest on its tail, much as kangaroos do today. Coelophysis might even have slept in a sitting-down position.

From footprints in rock and from fossil skeletons we have been able to learn a lot about Coelophysis and other dinosaurs. But there are some things that bones and footprints just can't tell us. They can't tell us what color Coelophysis or any other dino-saur might have been. Coelophysis may have been brightly colored, as many small lizards and snakes are today. Or it may have been dull green or brown, as many alligators and crocodiles are. We are pretty sure that the dinosaurs saw things in color, as we do, and some of them may have had patterns of color on their skins that helped them blend into the vegetation and hide from their enemies. But we don't know this for sure.

And we don't know whether Coelophysis or any other dinosaur made noises. It might have hissed, as many snakes and lizards do. It might have croaked or grunted or bel-lowed. It might have screeched like a big bird. Or maybe dinosaurs couldn't make any noise at all.

We don't know these things and we prob-ably never shall. For no human ever saw or heard a live dinosaur and never will. The last dinosaurs were all dead and gone more than 60 million years before man's earliest ancestors came shuffling into the world.

Apatosaurus — THE HARMLESS GIANT

THE AIR shimmers with heat above a small, shallow lake. Dragonflies dart and dodge about. From time to time there's a sudden splash, followed by a spread of ripples over the blue-green water as some strange, square-scaled fish hurls itself out of the water to gulp a passing insect in midair.

In the shallow water near the shore an animal is silently standing. It is simply enormous! Its huge, bulky body is supported by four massive legs as thick as old tree trunks. Now it shuffles ponderously up onto the bank, and the ground seems to shiver under the tread of those giant, barrellike feet. The creature's snaky neck is as long as a boa constrictor's whole body, and when it lifts that long neck up to peer suspiciously about, its blunt head is higher than most of the nearby trees!

The lakes and streams and swamps that dotted the land 150 million years ago were the homes of many creatures such as this. These giants were the biggest of all the dinosaurs and the biggest animals that have ever lumbered upon the land. They were plant eaters that walked on four legs, and we call them the sauropod dinosaurs.

One of the best known of these sauropods is the dinosaur that many people called Brontosaurus. But that isn't its right name. Scientists call it *Apatosaurus,* which means "unreal lizard" or "untrue lizard."

Perhaps Apatosaurus got its name because the scientist who found it couldn't believe it was real! From the end of its lengthy tail to the tip of its nose, Apatosaurus was about 70 feet long—almost as long as a whole passenger coach on a railroad train. It was about 15 feet high at the shoulder and weighed as much as five full-grown elephants. It was a living, moving mountain of bone, flesh, and muscle!

But for all its great size, Apatosaurus, like all the other sauropods, was quite harmless. Its teeth were blunt and weak and not good for anything but chewing the softest sorts of plants that grew in water. Apatosaurus probably spent most of its life —which may have been as long as 200 years—standing or wading in shallow lakes and streams, just eating. Down into the water would go the long neck, then up it would come again, with a big mass of greenery hanging out of each side of the mouth. As this was slowly munched, the

Rhamphorhync

APATOSAURUS

Rhamphorhynchus

head turned this way and that, making sure no enemy lurked nearby. And when the mouthful of plants was swallowed, down into the water went the head again. It took a lot of plants to fill that big stomach. So Apatosaurus's head was probably going up and down most of the time! Apatosaurus feeding must have looked a lot like one of those big machines that do nothing but scoop up dirt all day where a new building is being put up.

This sounds like a rather dull life, but Apatosaurus didn't know the difference. Its brain probably wasn't much bigger than that of a newborn kitten, and Apatosaurus may not even have been as smart as a newborn kitten. In fact, Apatosaurus had to have a sort of "second brain" to help the first one. This second brain was located on Apatosaurus's back, just where the tail began. There's a well-known, humorous poem that describes this unusual arrangement:

Behold the mighty dinosaur
Famous in prehistoric lore
Not only for his power and strength
But for his intellectual length.
You will observe by his remains
The creature had two sets of brains—
One in his head (the usual place),
The other at his spinal base. . . .
No problem bothered him a bit
He made both head and tail of it.
So wise was he, so wise and solemn,
Each thought filled just a spinal column.
If one brain found the pressure strong
It passed a few ideas along.
If something slipped his forward mind
'Twas rescued by the one behind.
And if in error he was caught
He had a saving afterthought.

As he thought twice before he spoke
He had no judgment to revoke.
Thus he could think without congestion
Upon both sides of every question. . . .

Actually, Apatosaurus's "second brain" was a kind of booster that simply helped the hind legs to work. Even with its two "brains," Apatosaurus was no smarter than any other dinosaur . . . and probably not even as smart as some.

Another unusual thing about Apatosaurus was the location of its nostrils. They weren't on its nose. They were on top of its head. With this kind of arrangement, Apatosaurus may have been able to go into quite deep water and stay there as long as it wished. By stretching its long neck straight up and keeping only the top of its head above water, Apatosaurus may have been able to stand in water 25 or 30 feet deep.

If Apatosaurus could do that, it would have had a good way of protecting itself. The forests that surrounded the streams and lakes where Apatosaurus lived were the hunting grounds of ferocious flesh-eating dinosaurs that loved nothing better than Apatosaurus meat. Allosaurus, Megalosaurus, and Ceratosaurus were dagger-toothed killers, and big though it was, Apatosaurus was helpless against them. But if Apatosaurus was near water when one of the hungry flesh eaters appeared, it would have been safe if it went into deep enough water. The flesh eaters couldn't get at it and probably couldn't even see it, with only the top of its head sticking out of the water.

Apatosaurus wasn't the only kind of sau-

Diplodocus

ropod. Many kinds of these big creatures lived together on the prehistoric lowland plains, just as many kinds of antelope now live on the plains of Africa. Some sauropods were bigger than others, and some had more teeth than others, but they were all shaped the same way. They all had big bodies and long, long necks and tails. And, like Apatosaurus, they all had their nostrils on the tops of their heads and they all spent most of their lives in water.

One of the smallest sauropods was Camarasaurus. From nose to tail tip it was only about 40 feet long. That's more than four times as long as the biggest elephant now alive, but compared to its huge cousin Apatosaurus, Camarasaurus was a runt.

But Apatosaurus wasn't the biggest or longest of all the sauropods. The title of longest dinosaur goes to the sauropod called Diplodocus, which was nearly 90 feet long. Despite its greater length, however, Diplodocus weighed much less than Apatosaurus because it was much less bulky.

Probably the biggest sauropod and the biggest of all dinosaurs was the giant Brachiosaurus. It was different from Apatosaurus, Diplodocus, and Camarasaurus in that its front legs were longer than the back ones, so it was shaped somewhat like a giraffe. In one museum there is a fossil bone from a brachiosaur's front leg that is taller than a tall man and thick enough for you to hide behind, as you might hide behind a thick tree! The brachiosaur this bone came from must have been about 20 feet high at the shoulders, and its head must have reached about 40 feet into the air. It could have looked over the top of a three-story building!

And yet, even Brachiosaurus may not have been the biggest member of the sauropod family. Fossil bones have been found that may have belonged to an even bigger sauropod! There weren't quite enough fossils to be absolutely sure, but this animal, which has been named Titanosaurus, may have been more than 100 feet long. That would make it the biggest animal that has ever lived on land or in the sea!

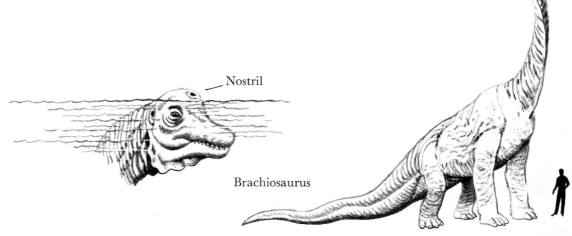

Nostril

Brachiosaurus

Comparative Size of a Six-foot Man

19

Stegosaurus—THE ROOFED DINOSAUR

ALL THE DINOSAURS were strange-looking creatures. But surely the strangest of all was Stegosaurus, a dinosaur that lived in North America about 150 million years ago.

For one thing, when you look at a picture of Stegosaurus or at its fossil skeleton, you wonder how such a big animal could have such a tiny head. Stegosaurus's body was about 20 feet long and weighed about 2 tons, but its narrow, birdlike head was only 16 inches long. The brain in that head weighed only about 2 ounces and was no bigger than a walnut.

For another thing, Stegosaurus's back legs were more than twice as long as its front ones. Thus, while its nose was nearly touching the ground, its rear end was nearly 8 feet in the air. No other dinosaur was quite as oddly shaped.

Lastly, and perhaps the strangest feature of all, up Stegosaurus's back and down most of its tail marched a double row of bony plates that looked like the spades in a deck of playing cards. The plates on Stegosaurus's neck were small, but they got bigger the farther back they went, until those at the hips were 2 feet high. Each plate was about 2 inches thick and covered with tough, horny skin.

Stegosaurus gets its name from these strange bony plates. Professor O. C. Marsh, who first discovered fossils of Stegosaurus, felt that the bony plates looked like roof shingles. So he gave the animal its name, which means "roofed lizard."

The pointed plates on Stegosaurus's back present scientists with two puzzles. First, just exactly how did these bony plates fit onto the animal's back? When Stegosaurus's fossil skeleton was first discovered, it was thought that the plates ran in a single row along its back. But it was soon seen that there were too many of the plates for that to have been the case. Scientists then decided that the plates must have run in two rows, side by side. But that didn't seem right either, because all the plates are different sizes.

Then, a fossil Stegosaurus skeleton was found which seemed to show that the plates ran up Stegosaurus's back in a zigzag pattern—a small plate on the left, then a little bigger one on the right, then a still bigger one on the left, and so on. Most scientists now think that this was probably the way the plates were arranged. But there is still some doubt.

But there is an even more puzzling problem: What were the bony plates on Stego-

Ceratosaurus

STEGOSAURUS

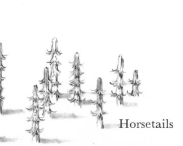

Horsetails

saurus's back *for*? They certainly weren't just decorations, because nearly every part of every animal's body has some reason for being where and what it is. But no animal living today has anything like those spade-shaped plates, so there's no way of telling just how Stegosaurus made use of them.

Some scientists think that perhaps the plates protected Stegosaurus by keeping flesh-eating dinosaurs from leaping onto its back. But the points of the plates don't look as if they would have been sharp enough to bother a really hungry flesh eater. And besides, the plates were just held in place by Stegosaurus's skin. They probably would have bent over if another dinosaur leaned its heavy body on them, and so would not have been much protection.

Another guess is that maybe the bony points were a means of frightening meat eaters away. The little frilled lizard that lives in Australia today has a big flap of skin around its neck which lifts up when the lizard is in danger. This makes the lizard look suddenly bigger and frightens its enemies away. Some scientists have suggested that Stegosaurus's bony plates behaved the same way. Maybe they lay flat most of the time and only stood up when Stegosaurus was in danger, to make it look bigger. But would this have been enough to frighten off a 34-foot-long Allosaurus that often hunted 70-foot-long apatosaurs? It doesn't seem likely.

Perhaps the bony plates somehow helped Stegosaurus to hide. We know from the shape of its 100 blunt teeth that Stegosaurus ate plants, and we know that it prob-

ably stayed among trees on flat ground because its head was too low for it to be able to wade in swamps. So maybe the shape and color of Stegosaurus's bony plates helped it blend into the forest background so that flesh eaters couldn't see it very well.

But all these ideas are really just guesses. No one knows for sure what the bony plates were for.

Stegosaurus's tail was 10 feet long—about half the length of the animal's whole body. It was a thick, powerful tail, and sticking up from the end of it were two pairs of enormous, hornlike spikes, each nearly a yard long. Maybe we don't know for sure what Stegosaurus's bony back plates were for, but there's not much doubt about what those big spikes were for. Stegosaurus's tail was a war club!

It's easy to imagine how the ancient reptile used its tail to defend itself. Picture a forest filled with feathery-leafed palms and ferns and lacy ginkgo trees. A bulky stegosaur is moving among the trees. It stops from time to time to clip a mouthful of greenery from the top of a low-growing plant. Slowly, it makes its way to a clearing through which flows a narrow stream. The big animal lowers its tiny, birdlike head and begins to gulp water.

Suddenly, out of the trees on the other side of the stream stalks a big, two-legged reptile. Its wide mouth bristles with sharp teeth, and the four-fingered hands on its forelegs are tipped with savage talons. On the beast's nose is a stubby horn. A flesh-eating Ceratosaurus!

The flesh eater hurls itself across the

22

stream, its taloned feet sending up splashes. The stegosaur jerks its head out of the water and clumsily moves away. But it keeps its body twisted around so that its tail is toward the attacking Ceratosaurus.

The Ceratosaurus charges forward. As it does so, the stegosaur swings its tail viciously, slamming it into the flesh eater. The Ceratosaurus is sent staggering, its flank marked with several deep, bloody gashes made by the spikes on the stegosaur's tail! Once more the Ceratosaurus tries to close in and sink its teeth and claws into the stegosaur's flesh. Again a blow from the plant eater's tail knocks the flesh eater reeling, with new bloody welts on its body. Now, moving as quickly as it can, the stegosaur makes its way into the safety of the trees. Dazed and in pain from its frightful wounds, the Ceratosaurus stares after it for a few moments, then limps sullenly off.

Fossil bones of Stegosaurus have been found in North America and England, and bones of Stegosaurus's relatives have been found in many other parts of the world. Kentrosaurus was an African stegosaur that was a little smaller than its American cousin and had fewer bony plates and more spikes on its tail. Chialingosaurus was a stegosaur that lived in eastern Asia. Fossil bones and even some eggs of a stegosaur named Omosaurus have been found in several parts of Europe. All these animals lived at about the same time.

All this tells us that stegosaurs were plentiful in the world of 150 million years ago. Scientists would say that animals that were this widespread were "successful" and should have been around for a long time. And yet, the stegosaurs all died off and vanished many millions of years before any of the other kinds of dinosaurs did. Why this happened we don't know. It's just another one of the many mysteries connected with those most mysterious creatures, the dinosaurs.

Allosaurus—THE HUNTER OF GIANTS

THE FOREST is thick and green and gloomy and silent. The air is hot and damp. Tiny beads of water drip steadily from the little fan-shaped leaves of sweating ginkgo trees and patter softly on the ground. The only sound or movement is the occasional buzz and flash of a winged insect darting through the green shadows.

But then, farther back in the forest, something moves—a huge, two-legged shape among the trees. The sound of its heavy feet padding in the mud breaks the forest silence. The creature moves out of the shadows into a patch of sunlight and stands for a moment, turning its head sharply from side to side as it peers about.

It is a huge, fearful reptile! Its 2½-foot-long head is split by an enormous mouth that seems to grin, showing rows of sharp, curved, 3-inch teeth. Its hands are 3-fingered, and on each finger is a razor-sharp talon. From its nose to the end of its long, powerful tail it is 34 feet long and stands nearly 10 feet high. It is a monstrous, frightening animal, like a dragon in a legend!

This was Allosaurus, the terrible flesh-eating dinosaur that roamed the plains and stream beds of western North America

about 150 million years ago. It was a fierce killer, ruling its part of the ancient world just as lions and tigers rule their parts of the world now.

Small flesh-eating dinosaurs ate small animals, and big flesh-eating dinosaurs ate big animals. Allosaurus was the biggest flesh-eating dinosaur of its time, and it ate some of the biggest of all animals. Its main source of food was the flesh of the long-necked, 70-foot-long Apatosaurus that weighed as much as several elephants. We know for sure that Allosaurus ate Apatosaurus because fossil Apatosaurus bones have been found with the marks of Allosaurus teeth in them. And at least one Allosaurus, feasting on Apatosaurus flesh, bit so fiercely and hungrily into its prey that some of its teeth broke off! They were found among the apatosaur's bones.

When Allosaurus went hunting it probably prowled along slowly, slightly crouched, with its tail dragging behind it. But when prey was sighted, Allosaurus bent its body forward, lifted its tail into the air, and ran. It probably couldn't run very fast or very far without tiring, but it was more than quick enough to catch up with a heavy, lumbering apatosaur that might

ALLOSAURUS

Apatosaurus

Theriosuchus

Camptosaurus

have ventured out of the safety of the deep water in its lagoon home. When Allosaurus caught up with its victim it probably stretched its head forward and clamped wicked teeth in the unfortunate animal's neck, hurling itself onto the apatosaur's back to bring it to the ground. Allosaurus probably had to bite and claw at a big apatosaur for a while in order to kill it, but a small dinosaur, such as a camptosaur, probably died as soon as Allosaurus's teeth met in its throat.

When its prey was no longer struggling, Allosaurus began to feed. It stood with its tail stretched out straight, for balance, and with the top part of its body bent forward so that its clawed hands were resting on the victim's body. The flesh eater sank its teeth into the dead dinosaur and then pulled and tugged and jerked its head until a huge chunk of flesh tore away. Allosaurus gulped such chunks down without chewing. It was able to swallow pieces of meat which were nearly as big as its whole mouth because, like a snake, the bones of its head could come apart slightly so that the whole head stretched.

Some scientists have suggested that Allosaurus didn't really hunt and kill its food, but simply ate dead animals it found as it wandered from place to place. But most scientists think that any animal with teeth and claws as sharp as those of Allosaurus must have been a fierce hunter and killer. And some fossils have been found that certainly seem to show that Allosaurus really did hunt the big Apatosaurus.

These fossils are footprints that were found in a Texas riverbed in 1940. Some of them were made when an apatosaur or one of the other gigantic sauropods sloshed along through a shallow stream. Its big feet sank into the mud, leaving clear tracks that hardened into stone over millions of years. And right alongside the apatosaur's tracks, pointed in the same direction, are the footprints of an Allosaurus or a big meat-eating dinosaur like it. It seems clear that the Allosaurus *was* hunting the other dinosaur, because where the apatosaur's tracks swerve suddenly to the left, so do the Allosaurus's footprints. It looks as if the apatosaur, aware that it was being followed by the flesh eater, moved into the middle of the stream, hoping to find deeper water. But the water was still shallow enough for the Allosaurus to keep wading after the big plant eater.

There's no way of telling from these tracks how far apart the two animals were, but they were probably able to see each other. We can imagine the apatosaur twisting its long neck to look anxiously back at its pursuer and the Allosaurus splashing along with its horrible, grinning mouth and its clawed hands twitching eagerly. We don't know if the apatosaur got away or if the flesh eater finally caught up with it. But isn't it exciting to think about these two huge creatures splashing through that long-ago stream and leaving footprints which lasted more than a hundred million years to tell us the story of that long-ago hunt.

Allosaurus had a smaller cousin that also lived in North America, but about 130 mil-

Ceratosaurus

lion years ago. It is called Ceratosaurus, and it was 17 feet long and about 8 feet high, with a 20-inch head and 2-inch teeth. It looked like a small Allosaurus except that it had a sort of bony knob above each eye and a short horn on the end of its nose.

It's a little hard to imagine what that horn could have been used for. Most animals that have horns use them for protection. But Ceratosaurus's sharp teeth and claws were certainly protection enough. And besides, since Ceratosaurus was a flesh eater, *it* didn't need protection—other dinosaurs needed protection from it! Nor would Ceratosaurus have had to use its horn when it attacked its prey. Its teeth and claws were more than sufficient. So we really don't know why Ceratosaurus had that horn on its nose.

Allosaurus had other relatives living in many parts of the world. One of these was Megalosaurus, which lived in England and possibly in other parts of Europe as well.

Megalosaurus was smaller than Allosaurus—about 20 feet long and 12 feet high. But otherwise it looked much like its American cousin. It is quite a famous dinosaur among scientists because it was Megalosaurus's fossil bones that were the first dinosaur fossils to be studied, and Megalosaurus was the first dinosaur to be given a name. You might think that the first dinosaur known would have been given a very special, fancy name. But all that *Megalosaurus* means is "large lizard."

And what about Allosaurus? Does this huge, savage monster have a name that's worthy of the most ferocious flesh eater of its time? Not at all! It's hard to imagine why the man who named Allosaurus chose the name he did—for *Allosaurus* means simply "other lizard."

Present-day Iguana

Iguanodon — THE MOST FAMOUS DINOSAUR

THERE WAS once a party held inside a dinosaur!

Of course, it wasn't a real dinosaur. It was a model—a life-size model of a dinosaur called Iguanodon. The model was hollow, and at a table that had been placed inside it, 22 men had a dinner party. The men were all scientists who were interested in dinosaurs, and the party was in honor of the most famous dinosaur of the time—none other than Iguanodon itself.

Iguanodon was famous because it was the first dinosaur that people really knew anything about. Until about 150 years ago, no one knew that there were such things as dinosaurs. People knew about fossil bones and footprints, but they thought that the bones belonged to long-dead elephants or other large animals, and that the footprints had been made by big birds. No one had the slightest idea that giant reptiles had once roamed the world.

Then, one March morning in 1822, Mrs. Gideon Mantell, the wife of an English doctor, went for a walk in the country. As she passed a pile of rocks, something caught her eye. It seemed to be a huge tooth, buried in a piece of rock. Mrs. Mantell picked up the rock and took it home to show her husband.

Dr. Mantell collected fossils for fun, and he knew a lot about them. But he had never seen anything like this tooth. He couldn't imagine what kind of animal might have had such teeth in its jaws. He began to spend all his spare time searching among the rocks where his wife had found the tooth, hoping to find more fossils from the same animal. His efforts were rewarded, for he found several more teeth and some fossil bones as well.

He showed these fossils to several scientists who told him that the teeth belonged to an ancient rhinoceros and the bones to an extinct hippopotamus. But then he chanced to show the fossil teeth to a man who had spent many years studying the iguana, a lizard of Mexico and Central America.

"Why," said the man, "they look just like an iguana's teeth. Only, they are much, much bigger!"

Dr. Mantell was now sure he had discovered a new kind of animal—a giant plant-eating lizard that had lived many years ago. He named the animal *Iguano-*

don, which means "iguana tooth," and he wrote a description of what he thought it must have been like.

Just about the same time, another scientist published a description of some fossil bones he had been studying. He had decided that they were the bones of a giant flesh-eating lizard (Megalosaurus). Most other scientists agreed with him. And they also agreed that Dr. Mantell's fossils belonged to a different kind of lizard giant that had lived at the same time as the flesh eater. Dinosaurs had been discovered!

Other dinosaur fossils were soon found, and people everywhere became excited and curious about these strange animals of long ago. Scientists began to try to puzzle out what the creatures had looked like, and in 1853 a sculptor with the odd name of Waterhouse Hawkins decided to make a life-size model of a dinosaur. He picked the dinosaur that scientists seemed to know the most about—Dr. Mantell's Iguanodon. And that's how Iguanodon became famous.

The model that Mr. Hawkins built was the very same model in which the 22 scientists had their dinner party. It now stands in a park in the city of London, and people who know a lot about dinosaurs smile when they see it, for it doesn't look much like a dinosaur—it looks like a fat rhinoceros with scales and a long tail. That's because the scientists who first studied dinosaurs thought Iguanodon was simply a giant iguana lizard, and because a short, sharp horn found among some Iguanodon fossils led them to believe that Iguanodon had a horn on its nose. Scientists also thought that

Iguanodon was much bigger than it really was, which is why the model is big enough for 22 men to be able to sit in it.

For many years it was thought that the model showed pretty much how Iguanodon had really looked. Then, in 1877, some coal miners in Belgium made a wonderful discovery. Right where they were digging, a stream had run through a narrow gully millions of years before. Mud, dead plants, and dead animals were carried by the flowing water and piled up all together at places along the riverbank. As the miners dug a new tunnel, they came to just such a place and found the skeletons of 23 dinosaurs. The skeletons were all of the same kind of dinosaur, and scientists soon realized what dinosaurs these creatures had been—iguanodonts!

All those skeletons showed the scientists what Iguanodon had *really* looked like, and it wasn't much like Mr. Hawkins's model. Iguanodon was not a four-footed animal as everyone had thought. It walked upright on its two back legs. And it didn't have a horn on its nose—both of its "thumbs" were horns!

From those skeletons and from fossil footprints and even from prints of skin, we now know more about Iguanodon than we do about most other dinosaurs. It lived about 100 million years ago in what is now England, continental Europe, and North Africa. It was a bulky, good-sized dinosaur that weighed about 7 tons, and was about 15 feet high and more than 30 feet long. As Dr. Mantell had seen by the shape of its teeth, it was a plant eater. Some scientists think it

Ginkgo

may have had a long tongue, like that of a giraffe, with which it pulled twigs into its mouth, snipped the tops off with the sharp, bony front of its jaws, and ground them to a pulp between its rows of teeth.

Iguanodon's hands were much like human hands. Iguanodon probably used them to hold on to the branches from which it was munching leaves. But the thumbs of those hands were short, sharp spikes, like horns, and most scientists think they were used as weapons. Maybe if Iguanodon was attacked by a flesh-eating dinosaur, it used its sharp thumbs like daggers and jabbed them into its enemy's belly!

Although Iguanodon was a big, heavy dinosaur, we can tell from some of its tracks that it could move quite fast if it wanted to. When it ran, it lifted its tail off the ground and bent its body far forward. And from some of the tracks we can see that when Iguanodon got tired it leaned back and sat on its tail.

Iguanodon belonged to a group of dinosaurs that are called *ornithopods,* which means "bird feet." We know a lot about the other dinosaurs in this group—Iguanodon's ancestors and descendants.

Camptosaurus, an American ornithopod that lived many millions of years earlier than Iguanodon, was probably an ancestor. It looked just about like Iguanodon but was much smaller—only averaging about 15 feet long and 7 or 8 feet high. An even smaller ancestor was Hypsilophodon, a dinosaur that looked like an Iguanodon but was only about 5 feet long and 2 feet high.

Some of Iguanodon's descendants were the hadrosaurs, or duck-billed dinosaurs. Another descendant was an extremely odd dinosaur with the jawbreaking name of Pachycephalosaurus. That means "thick-headed lizard," which is a good name because the top of this strange creature's head swelled up into a big bump of solid bone as much as 10 inches thick! And all around this bump, and on the dinosaur's nose, there were clusters of small, bony knobs and spikes.

What could these thick bone heads have been for? It's a puzzle to scientists, because no animal living today has such a head. But maybe these dinosaurs used their thick skulls the same way that billy goats do—maybe they fought with each other at mating time by banging their heads together!

Hypsilophodon

Pachycephalosaurus

31

Compsognathus — THE SMALLEST DINOSAUR

THE VERY WORD "dinosaur" makes most people think of something huge and fearsome. It conjures up thoughts of a gigantic, scaly monster, lumbering through steamy jungles with its head reaching higher than the treetops. But while this description fits some of the dinosaurs, it certainly doesn't fit all of them, for many of the dinosaurs were quite small. One of them, in fact, was actually tiny.

About 150 million years ago, at the same time creatures like 34-foot-long Allosaurus were stalking the swamps in search of a 70-foot-long apatosaur, a tiny reptile no bigger than a chicken was also scurrying about among the ginkgoes and cycads. It had a 3-inch-long head on a long, slender neck, and its tail was longer than its head, neck, and body all together. It ran swiftly on its two back legs. This little animal was a dinosaur—the smallest dinosaur of all, as far as we know. Its name is Compsognathus.

What sort of life did this tiny beast live in a world full of giants? It probably trotted about on the muddy shores of shallow lakes in search of smaller reptiles and large insects to eat, for we can tell by the sharp, little teeth in Compsognathus's fossil skull that it was a meat eater. But it probably wasn't too fussy about the things it ate. If it chanced to come across a long-dead fish or shellfish that had been cast up on the shore, it gladly feasted on it.

The best fossil skeleton of Compsognathus was found in Bavaria, Germany, in stone that had once been lagoon mud. But there's a mystery connected with this skeleton. Inside it, right where Compsognathus's stomach would have been, there seems to be another skeleton—the skeleton of what appears to be a very tiny reptile.

Could this have been a *baby* Compsognathus? Some scientists think so. They think that Compsognathus may not have laid eggs as most other dinosaurs seem to have done, but that it had its babies the same way mammals do. But most scientists think this tiny skeleton is just the skeleton of some smaller animal that Compsognathus swallowed whole.

Most of the little animals that Compsognathus saw and hunted were much like animals that live today—lizards, turtles, and various kinds of insects. But as Compsognathus scurried about on the banks of its little lagoon world, it may have seen two other small creatures which, although they

Pterodactyl

COMPSOGNATHU

Dapedius

were not dinosaurs, were not like any animal living today.

One was a flying reptile—like a lizard with wings! It is called Pterodactylus. Scientists think it probably lived among trees on the edge of lagoons where Compsognathus also lived.

Some pterodactyls were as big as squirrels, and some were no bigger than a sparrow. Their wings were like thin flaps of leather attached to their arms and body. A Pterodactyl's jaws were long and pointed, like a bird's beak, and were filled with sharp, wickedly curved, little teeth. There were claws on its wings and feet, which probably helped it scramble up a tree trunk as easily as a squirrel does.

In many ways Pterodactyl was like a bird even though it wasn't at all related to birds. Its bones were hollow, as a bird's bones are, and it was probably warm-blooded, like birds and mammals. This means it was very active, not at all slow and sluggish as reptiles often are. On its flimsy wings it soared and glided over the lagoon, swooping down to snatch up tiny fish and perhaps snapping up insects in midair. Because of the way its wings were shaped, some scientists think it may have slept as bats do, hanging head down from a branch with its wings wrapped around itself.

We don't know what Pterodactyl's skin looked like, but we do know that it had no feathers. Its skin may have been scaly, or smooth, or perhaps even *hairy*, because some fossils of this curious creature seem to show a sort of fur on the body. If this is so, Pterodactyl must certainly wear the crown

Pterodactyl

as the strangest and most mixed-up animal that has ever lived: a warm-blooded reptile with wings, a bird's beak filled with teeth, and fur like a mammal!

The other creature that may have lived near the lagoon along with Compsognathus was also winged. But unlike Pterodactyl, this animal had feathers. It was a winged reptile with feathers—a reptile that was evolving into a bird!

This creature is called *Archaeopteryx,* which means "ancient wing," and it was really the first kind of bird in the world. The fossil skeletons of Archaeopteryx provide positive evidence that reptiles are the ancestors of birds, for Archaeopteryx had 17 feathers on each wing, and feathers on its legs, body, and tail. But its head was a little reptile head, and instead of a beak, it had jaws full of little, needle-sharp teeth. Its tail, beneath the feathers, was a long, snaky reptile tail. And on each of the wings was a little, clawed reptile hand. Like Pterodactyl, Archaeopteryx could climb trees.

Even though it had feathers, Archaeopteryx probably wasn't a very good flyer, perhaps not even as good a flyer as Pterodactyl. Its wings were far too weak to have gotten it off the ground, so it must have flown by hopping out of high trees and spreading its wings to simply glide and soar. It probably didn't do much wing flapping.

This means that if Archaeopteryx had to alight on the ground for any reason, it must have been helpless until it could waddle to the nearest tree and climb to safety. There may have been times when an Archaeop-

34

Archaeopteryx

teryx was trapped on the ground and could not move fast enough to escape the sharp, little teeth of a Compsognathus that happened by. Archaeopteryx was no bigger than a pigeon, so Compsognathus could probably have easily overcome it.

It sounds as if Compsognathus was the undisputed king of its little world, living off smaller, more helpless creatures and having an easy time of it. But this may not have been the case, for even though Compsognathus was a flesh eater, its own small size made it fair game for bigger flesh eaters. Giant Allosaurus or Megalosaurus probably wouldn't have noticed such a tiny creature. But there were other flesh eaters that were only two or three times bigger than Compsognathus, and it would have been just the right size to make a hearty meal for one of them!

These other small flesh eaters were members of Compsognathus's own family, the coelurosaurs. They were fast-moving reptiles, about 6 feet long and 3 feet high, with slender, fingerlike claws they probably used for grabbing up quick, little creatures that skittered over the ground. One of these coelurosaurs that lived in North America has been named *Ornitholestes,* which means "bird catcher," because some scientists think it may have been quick enough to leap up and grab birds out of the air if they swooped too low. But this is most doubtful.

Despite their small size, these flesh-eating coelurosaurs were widespread and successful dinosaurs. Their fossil bones have been found in North and South America, Asia, Africa, and Australia, and little three-toed footprints made by some of them have been found in England.

And some of them lived in continental Europe where, from time to time, they may have dined on their cousin Compsognathus, the smallest of them all.

Unfolding Ferns

Ornitholestes

Anatosaurus — THE DUCK-BILLED DINOSAUR

IF YOU could have stood on the shore of most any North American lagoon about 80 million years ago, sooner or later you might have seen what seemed to be a huge duck swimming toward you. But as it neared the shore and stood up to wade out of the water on its two hind legs, you would have seen that it was a dinosaur— a dinosaur with a long, narrow head and jaws shaped remarkably like the bill of a duck or goose.

Scientists call this odd creature *Anatosaurus,* which means "goose lizard." But it's more commonly called a duck-billed dinosaur. Eighty million years ago duck-billed dinosaurs, or hadrosaurs, were one of the most common kinds of dinosaurs in North America.

You can expect to find ducks near water, so perhaps it's not too surprising that duck-billed dinosaurs spent most of their time in and around water, too. Anatosaurus lumbered about on sandy riverbanks and lakeshores, looking for food. It walked upright on its two sturdy back legs, but often it dropped to all four feet to shovel in the mud with its broad, ducklike bill in search of tasty roots and bulbs and perhaps a snail or two. Its favorite food may have

been rushes or cattails, plants that still grow near lakes and ponds to this day.

If food was scarce on the shore, Anatosaurus waded into the water, ducking down to peer about for juicy water plants. If that search proved in vain, Anatosaurus leaned forward in the water, gave a kick with its hind legs, and set off to swim to another part of the lake or another piece of shore where it might be able to find something to its taste.

Duck-billed dinosaurs were probably the champion swimmers of all the dinosaurs. Anatosaurus's front feet were webbed, like the feet of a duck or goose, and its powerful tail was flattened, like the tail of a crocodile. Anatosaurus swam by paddling with its webbed feet and moving its tail from side to side like a big oar. But it probably wasn't as graceful a swimmer as a modern crocodile or sea turtle. Anatosaurus must have swum more like a hippopotamus.

Water meant safety as well as food for Anatosaurus, for although it was a rather big dinosaur—about 30 feet long and 12 feet high—it had absolutely no way of defending itself. The claws on its webbed feet were small and blunt, no good at all for fighting, and the claws on its back feet

Cattails

ANATOSAURU

Turtle Lungfi

Present-day Gila Monster

were like blunt hooves. Its teeth weren't sharp enough to do any damage, and its skin, although tough and leathery, wasn't really much protection against the sharp teeth of some of the terrible flesh-eating dinosaurs that roamed hungrily about. So when Anatosaurus was peacefully browsing among the cattails and rushes, and Tyrannosaurus suddenly came stalking out of a forest, the poor duckbill had to scurry for the water and swim for its life! The flesh-eating dinosaurs weren't very good swimmers, so once Anatosaurus reached deep water it was safe.

We know a good deal more about Anatosaurus than we do about most other dinosaurs because of two wonderful mummy-like fossils of duck-billed dinosaurs that were found in Wyoming many years ago. These stone "mummies" show things that just plain fossil bones could never reveal, such as Anatosaurus's webbed feet and the sort of ruffle of thick skin that ran down the animal's back to the end of its tail. Best of all, one of the fossils was covered with a stone "picture" of its skin! It had been covered with soft mud that received an imprint of the skin, just as a coin leaves an imprint when it is pressed into modeling clay. Over millions of years the mud hardened into rock with the skin imprint still in it, showing what a duck-billed dinosaur's skin looked like.

The skin of Anatosaurus was thick and leathery and covered all over with tiny bumps mixed with little clusters of bigger bumps. Anatosaurus's skin was apparently very much like the skin of the little lizard called a Gila monster, which lives today in the same part of western North America where Anatosaurus lived those millions of years ago.

The other "mummy" tells us something about the place where an Anatosaurus lived and gives us a dramatic picture of how this dinosaur died. The anatosaur's body was stretched out full length with one leg reaching down and with its bill pointing straight up. The unfortunate animal had wandered into a patch of quicksand or into a deep, muddy bog and sank to its death, vainly trying to keep its head above the mud so it could breathe.

Anatosaurus wasn't the only kind of duck-billed dinosaur. There were many other kinds, all equally odd in appearance. Kritosaurus, Corythosaurus, and Lambeosaurus were three duckbills that lived millions of years before Anatosaurus, but they were all its relatives. Their bodies were shaped almost exactly like Anatosaurus's body, but their heads were quite different. Kritosaurus had a big bump on its nose that made its jaws look more like a parrot's beak than a duck's bill. Corythosaurus had a bony crest shaped like a half circle on its head. And on Lambeosaurus's head was a crest shaped like a hatchet!

Oddest of all when it came to fancy head decorations was Parasaurolophus, a duck-billed dinosaur that lived at about the same time as Anatosaurus. Parasaurolophus had a long, curved tube of bone that stuck far out of the back of its head.

Why did these duck-billed dinosaurs have such odd bumps and bony decorations

38

Corythosaurus

Lambeosaurus

on their heads? Was there a reason for them, or were they just for show? Most scientists think there was a reason, but they're not sure what it was. For one thing, all the bony crests were hollow, and tubes ran from them through the duckbills' skulls to their noses, so that when the duckbill took a breath, the air went up into its crest. Maybe the bony crests were air-storage chambers that helped the duck-billed dinosaurs stay under water longer while they fed. Or maybe the crests gave the duckbills a better sense of smell. That would have been a big help if a hungry Tyrannosaurus was coming their way.

And maybe these crests were noisemakers. Maybe they acted like trumpets, so that sounds the duckbills made echoed and sounded louder. Just imagine what hootings and bellowings these big animals might have made!

Anatosaurus didn't have a fancy ornament on its head as most of its relatives did. In fact, Anatosaurus is sometimes called a "flat-headed" duckbill. But there was one special feature that Anatosaurus shared with all other duckbills. Teeth! All these dinosaurs had hundreds of teeth!

Duckbills needed lots of teeth because of the way they ate. They ground tough plants to a pulp by rubbing them between their upper and lower teeth. All this grinding slowly wore the teeth down. By examining Anatosaurus skulls, scientists have found that a duckbill was always growing new teeth that pushed up to replace those that wore out. A duckbill such as Anatosaurus regularly used more than 2,000 teeth during its lifetime!

Even though Anatosaurus and its relatives were cold-blooded reptiles and giants in size, they seem to have been mild, inoffensive creatures. With their webbed feet dangling in front of them like the paws of a sleeping puppy and with their ducklike bills and large eyes, they must have had an almost gentle look. It's easy to imagine them in some long-ago lagoon, swimming and sloshing and snorting and hunting for good things to eat in the water they loved.

Parasaurolophus

Protoceratops — THE EGG LAYER

OUR KNOWLEDGE of dinosaurs is like a picture puzzle with a lot of missing pieces. Each missing piece is an unanswered question. But every once in a while a great discovery is made that lets us put a new piece into the puzzle.

In 1922 a group of American scientists in the Gobi desert of Mongolia found the fossil skull of a new kind of dinosaur. Its mouth was a hard, horny beak, like the beak of a parrot. Such a mouth was well designed for snipping off the tops of low-growing plants. Out of the back of the skull grew a curved, bony shield that must have spread back over the animal's neck. Scientists looked at this bony shield and the beaked jaws and named the new dinosaur Protoceratops.

Now *Protoceratops* means "first horned face." Why was such a name given to an animal that had no horns? Why wasn't this dinosaur called by a name that meant "shield head" or perhaps "parrot beak?" Actually, there was a good reason for scientists to name the animal as they did. They realized that this dinosaur was related to some other dinosaurs they had known about for a long time, a whole family of dinosaurs that had beaked mouths, bony shields growing out of their heads, and *horns*. These dinosaurs had been named *ceratopsians,* which means "horned faces." And Protoceratops was named *"first horned face"* because the scientists felt that Protoceratops probably looked very much like the first kinds of ceratopsian dinosaurs.

Finding a new dinosaur that belonged to a family of well-known dinosaurs was a great discovery that put an important piece into the picture puzzle of dinosaur knowledge. But even more was to come.

A year after the Protoceratops skull had been found, a small group of men—the same scientists who had found the skull—stood beside a sandstone cliff in the hot, parched Gobi desert. They were clustered around one man who held something in his hands—a creamy white object about the size and shape of a baked potato.

"Gentlemen," said the man, turning the thing over in his hands, "there is no doubt about it. You are looking at the first dinosaur egg ever found!"

These men had made one of the greatest discoveries in all the history of fossil hunting. For many years one of the biggest questions in the minds of most people who studied dinosaurs was, How were baby

Another Kind of Ceratopsian (Styracosaurus)

dinosaurs born? Since dinosaurs were reptiles, and most reptiles hatch from eggs, it was generally believed that dinosaur babies probably hatched from eggs, too. But there was no way to be sure of this, and it seemed as if there never would be—for it was hardly possible that such a fragile thing as an egg could leave any kind of trace after millions of years.

But now eggs had been found. There were about 20 of them, whole and in pieces, in a chunk of weathered red sandstone. This showed that dinosaurs not only laid eggs but laid them in nests, just as many modern reptiles do. And the scientists were even fairly sure they knew what kind of dinosaur had laid these eggs. It seemed to be none other than the dinosaur they had recently discovered—Protoceratops!

About 100 million years ago the Gobi desert was a flat, sandy plain dotted with small, scrubby plants. The mother Protoceratops hunted for a place to lay her eggs. She was a short, squat reptile, only about 6 feet long from the end of her tail to her beaked nose. Moving slowly along the edge of a small pond, she examined one sand dune after another. She wanted a place where the sand was neither too coarse nor too fine.

At last she found a dune that suited her. With her clawed, five-toed front feet, she scooped out a broad, shallow pit. Crouching over this, she began to lay her eggs.

One by one the eggs plopped into the pit until, after a time, about 20 of them lay clustered in three layers at the bottom. They looked like small, white baked pota-

toes. Their shells were leathery and covered with tiny wrinkles.

Kicking with her back legs, the mother Protoceratops shoveled sand into the pit until the eggs were loosely covered. Then, without a backward glance, she shuffled off toward a distant clump of plants from which she began to clip bunches of leaves with her beaked jaws.

The eggs in their sandy nest were already forgotten. The mother dinosaur would never return to them nor pay any more attention to them. They were unprotected except for their light covering of sand. If one of the many egg-eating dinosaurs that lived in the desert should discover the nest, many of the eggs would be dug up and sucked dry. But if all went well, the warmth of the sand, heated by the sun, would do the job of hatching the eggs. The baby dinosaurs would break out of their shells and dig their way out of the sand into the world. This was how all Protoceratops babies, and most other kinds of dinosaur babies, were born.

But these Protoceratops babies were never to know life. Across the desert a brisk wind began to blow. The air became filled with whirling particles of sand. The wind increased in power until the whole great plain resounded with its wailing shriek. Savagely the wind lifted up tons of loose sand and flung them through the air in a yellow cloud.

For hours the sandstorm raged. And when the wind finally sank to a whisper and then died away, the Protoceratops eggs were buried deep under several feet of sand. With no air able to reach through this thick blanket, the unborn babies died inside their eggs.

As the insides of the eggs began to dry up, the weight of the sand cracked the shells. Through those cracks sand trickled into the eggs, tightly filling the shells. Now the *shapes* of the eggs were preserved— they couldn't be mashed flat.

Years passed, then whole centuries. More sand, carried by years of blowing winds, piled atop the eggs and buried them ever deeper. Minerals, carried by trickles of water from infrequent rains, soaked slowly through the close-packed sand and reached the eggs. These minerals seeped through the cracks in the shells and reached the tiny bones of the unhatched baby dinosaurs. And very, very slowly, each microscopic bit of eggshell or bone was replaced by mineral that hardened into rock. In this way the eggs became perfect petrified copies of themselves—stone fossils that were the exact size and shape of the originals.

Centuries went by. Thousands of years went by. Millions of years went by. The red desert sand hardened into sandstone, encasing the eggs in solid rock.

More millions of years passed. Each day the wind blew, the sun burned down. Occasional rains lashed the soft rock. Slowly the sandstone wore away into cliffs and gullies. And, by chance, the eggs that had been deeply buried became exposed in the side of a cliff, awaiting discovery by that little group of scientists.

That discovery was only a beginning. The scientists found more than 70 eggs, together with complete skeletons of newly hatched, half-grown, and adult protoceratopsians. They even found skeletons of unhatched babies in some of the eggs that had broken open. It was one of the greatest fossil finds ever made—a life history of a dinosaur from egg to adult!

Other dinosaur eggs have since been found. But little Protoceratops will always be famous as the dinosaur that first showed us how dinosaur babies were born. That discovery put one of the biggest and most important pieces into our picture puzzle of dinosaur knowledge.

Triceratops—THE THREE-HORNED FACE

SEVENTY MILLION years ago, the western part of North America was about as warm and moist as Florida is today. There were great swamps and forests of palm trees mixed with ginkgoes, figs, and giant redwoods. And on the edges of the marshes where there were vast plains of high, grasslike plants, herds of four-footed dinosaurs browsed, like cows in a pasture.

They weren't very big dinosaurs, only about 20 feet long and 10 feet high—a little longer than a big elephant but not quite as tall. Their tails were short and heavy, and their legs were thick, with broad, flat feet to support the weight of their bodies. Their toes were clawed—three claws on the toes of their front feet and four on the back—but the claws were small and blunt, like little hooves.

These dinosaurs had enormous heads that were nearly a third as long as their whole bodies. And out of the backs of their heads grew big shields of bone that spread out to cover their necks and shoulders. Their jaws were curved like parrotbeaks and they browsed by cocking their heads to one side and snipping off the tops of plants with their beaked mouths, as neatly as you might snip flower stems with a scissors.

But the most striking thing about these bulky reptiles were the horns that stuck up from their heads—a sharp, 3-foot-long horn above each eye, and a short, thick horn that poked up from the nose. It is from these horns that this dinosaur gets the name *Triceratops,* which means "three-horned face."

Even though Triceratops was a harmless plant eater, those horns on its head weren't just for show. Triceratops used them. It was a fighter! We know this because scars and scratches that were made by the horns of other triceratopsians have been found on the bony shields of fossil Triceratops skulls. Male horned dinosaurs may have fought each other at times, just as deer, antelope, and other horned animals fight each other today. What a fearsome sight it must have been when two of these massive, 10-ton beasts charged headlong at each other, with the earth shivering beneath their thudding feet. They may have nipped at each other with their parrotbeaks as they dodged and sidestepped, jerking and twisting their big heads to jab and stab with their horns. Sometimes, apparently, they fought so viciously that one animal's horn would break against another's bony

Pteranodon

←——————— 27′ ———————→

shield, for a triceratops skull has been found with a broken horn that had healed and was shorter than the horn on the other side of the face.

Since we know for sure that Triceratops fought others of its own kind, we can be sure it would have fought just as savagely to defend itself from any flesh eater that attacked it. And chances are that such fights did take place, for Triceratops lived at the same time and in the same place as the biggest flesh-eating animal of all, the terrible Tyrannosaurus.

Tyrannosaurus was twice as big as Triceratops . . . twice as long and twice as tall. But Triceratops had an edge in weight, and it also had those wicked horns. Tyrannosaurus may well have hesitated to pit itself against Triceratops unless it was made reckless by hunger. A tyrannosaur that encountered a herd of triceratopsians probably paced back and forth, restlessly eyeing the plant eaters and trying to make up its dull mind whether or not it wanted to attack one of them.

Or the fight might well have been started by a triceratops, its own dull, reptilian mind slowly aroused to anger by the sight of the prowling enemy. We can imagine what such a fight was like . . . .

Hungrily, the big tyrannosaur strides in a wide circle around the cluster of horned dinosaurs. From time to time it pauses to glare at them, its long tail twitching angrily. The triceratopsians nearest the flesh eater lift their great heads, warily eyeing it in return.

Then abruptly, a large, male triceratops lowers its head, and with horns pointing forward, launches itself at the tyrannosaur like a modern army tank charging full speed at an enemy! The tyrannosaur moves aside as the horned dinosaur thunders past, but a horn grazes the flesh eater's leg.

The triceratops slows to a stop and quickly turns to face its foe. The tyrannosaur paces swiftly around the three-horned face, seeking to catch the plant eater off guard so it can leap upon its back, but the triceratops wheels its body around, keeping its fierce horns always pointed at the enemy.

Once again the triceratops hurls itself suddenly forward, and this time the tyrannosaur isn't quick enough. The horned dinosaur slams into the flesh eater, jerking its head upward savagely so that its two long horns rip deep into the tyrannosaur's belly! The impact lifts the flesh eater off its feet and hurls it backward to sprawl on the ground. Moving forward quickly, the triceratops jabs its horn again and again into the fallen tyrannosaur's body.

Of course, there were probably times when Tyrannosaurus was the victor in such a battle, times when Triceratops was too young or too old to put up enough of a fight to save itself. But in actuality, fights between Tyrannosaurus and Triceratops must have been a rarity. Just as the savage lion of our world stays out of the way of the husky, horned rhinoceros, so Tyrannosaurus probably seldom bothered any of the horned dinosaurs.

Triceratops was one of the last and biggest of the horned dinosaurs. It had a close relative, Torosaurus, that lived at about the same time and looked much like Triceratops except that its bony head shield was

46

higher and wider. Both these beasts came from a big family of horned dinosaurs that lived in North America for several million years.

Pentaceratops, which lived a few million years earlier than Triceratops and Torosaurus, looked much like them except that it was slightly smaller. Also, in addition to the three horns on the top of its head, it had a sort of horn on each side of its lower jaw. *Pentaceratops* means "five-horned face."

Another horned dinosaur called Monoclonius lived still earlier by a few million years. It had two small horns above its eyes and one very long horn on its nose, just the opposite of Triceratops. Styracosaurus also had a long horn on its nose. It had no horns at all above its eyes, but sticking up from the edges of its bony shield were six long, wickedly pointed spikes. Chasmosaurus, still another early horned dinosaur, had two short horns above its eyes and a single short horn on its nose.

Most kinds of dinosaurs that lived in America also lived in many other parts of the world. But nearly all the fossils of horned dinosaurs have been found only in the western part of North America. A few have been found in Asia, but none anywhere else. Apparently in that far-off time, there were natural barriers of some kind that kept the horned dinosaurs from spreading east into the eastern part of North America or west into Europe and Africa.

Thus it seems that the horned dinosaurs must have gotten their start either in Asia or western North America. But which? Asia and North America were connected by a bridge of land millions of years ago, so the ancestor of the horned dinosaurs might have come into America from Asia —or it might have gone into Asia from America.

Was Triceratops a native American? Or, like everyone living in America today, did it have ancestors that "came over from the old country?"

Chasmosaurus

Monoclonius

47

Tyrannosaurus—THE TERRIBLE KILLER

JUST STANDING in front of the fossil skeleton of the dinosaur called Tyrannosaurus rex is enough to give you the shivers, because it's easy to imagine what this monster looked like when it was alive. It was a creature out of a nightmare—the biggest, most powerful flesh-eating animal that has ever walked the earth and probably the most terrible killer as well!

Tyrannosaurus walked on its two strong, heavy back legs, and when standing upright, was about 20 feet high. A tall man would have reached only to its knee. Its powerful body was nearly 50 feet long and weighed about 7½ tons—longer than a railroad boxcar and about equal to the biggest kind of elephant. The claws on Tyrannosaurus's three-toed feet were about 8 inches long. Its huge head was nearly 5 feet long and its jaws were filled with inch-thick, 6-inch-long teeth, pointed like daggers and saw-toothed like the cutting edge of a steak knife.

Tyrannosaurus rex means "king tyrant lizard." A tyrant is a cruel and powerful ruler who has the power of life and death over his subjects. And Tyrannosaurus certainly fits that description. This fierce, giant reptile was the king of beasts in its ancient world, and almost any other dinosaur that crossed its path was marked for attack from those dagger-sharp teeth and terrible, tearing claws. For Tyrannosaurus must have been little more than a walking appetite. It would have taken a lot of meat to keep that big body going, so Tyrannosaurus probably spent nearly every waking moment hunting for food. When it made a kill it must have gorged itself until its stomach was bursting. Then it squatted down and slept. Hunt, kill, eat, sleep, and wake up to hunt again—that was the story of Tyrannosaurus's life.

The tyrant reptile king lived about 70 million years ago in the western part of North America. It was the biggest of all the flesh-eating dinosaurs in the world, but it wasn't the only one of its time. It had a sort of cousin called Albertosaurus (because its fossil bones were found in Alberta, Canada) that lived at about the same time and in the same part of the country as Tyrannosaurus. Albertosaurus looked much like Tyrannosaurus but was considerably smaller. And there was a very strange flesh-eating dinosaur named Spinosaurus that lived where Egypt is today. This creature, too, looked much like Tyrannosaurus, but

Tyrannosaurus

Comparative Size of a Six-foot Man

48

Anatosaurus

on its back was a huge fin as much as 6 feet high, shaped like the fin on the back of a sailfish. Most scientists think this fin may have helped keep Spinosaurus from getting too hot or too cool.

The North American Tyrannosaurus wasn't the only Tyrannosaurus in the world. A slightly different kind of Tyrannosaurus also lived in Mongolia.

The many different kinds of fossil dinosaur skeletons that have been found in North America tell us that Tyrannosaurus had a wide variety of creatures from which to choose its prey. On the plains browsed solitary armored dinosaurs and herds of horned dinosaurs, and in the swamps there were still a few long-necked sauropods and a lot of duck-billed dinosaurs. Tyrannosaurus probably regarded all of these animals as food, but some of them were probably more difficult prey than others. While the horned dinosaurs were plentiful, they could fight extremely well. The armored dinosaurs were protected. The big sauropods stayed out of reach in deep water. So the animals that Tyrannosaurus probably hunted most often were the duck-billed dinosaurs. They were large but helpless; a nice, plump, 30-foot-long duckbill would have made an easy and excellent meal for a hungry tyrannosaur.

When a tyrannosaur went hunting it stalked along, taking steps that measured nearly 14 feet each. Its tiny arms were held bent against its chest, and its huge jaws were open in a grin that showed its wicked teeth—a grin as terrible and menacing as the snarl of a hungry tiger. Let's take an imaginary trip back into the past and follow a tyrannosaur as it searches for food.

The longer the tyrannosaur hunts, the greater its hunger grows. Rounding a clump of redwood trees, it comes suddenly upon an armored ankylosaur. The armored dinosaur is much too slow to run, so it depends on its armor to save it. Quickly it squats down, tucking its legs under itself.

The tyrannosaur bends low and snaps at the ankylosaur's armored back. Its teeth make a rasping sound against the hard, bony armor. The tyrannosaur claws at the ankylosaur with one of its big, taloned feet. But the armored dinosaur's broad, flat body hugs the ground like a boulder, and the tyrannosaur's claws barely scratch the armor.

The tyrannosaur is ravenously hungry now, and it becomes enraged. It bites again at the ankylosaur's back. Then suddenly, from among the trees where a broad river winds through the plain, there is a sound of splashing and snorting. The tyrannosaur's head jerks up and it glares toward the river. The flesh eater knows those sounds. There is prey near the river that will be easier to overcome than the ankylosaur!

Leaving the armored dinosaur still crouched in its tracks, the tyrannosaur lopes toward the sounds. On the riverbank three duck-billed anatosaurs, dripping from their swim in the river, are browsing about in search of the soft plants they enjoy. Suddenly, the tyrannosaur bursts through the trees.

The duckbills scatter as quickly as they

can, scrambling desperately toward the water in which they will be safe. But one duckbill is too late and too slow. In three strides the tyrannosaur has caught up with it. The flesh eater's enormous mouth gapes wider for an instant, then the fierce teeth crunch into the back of the duckbill's neck. The weight of the tyrannosaur's body crushes the duckbill to the ground. With a savage wrench of its jaws, the flesh eater nearly severs the duckbill's head from its body.

Now the tyrannosaur squats down so that its huge body is nearly lying across that of the dead anatosaur. It sinks its teeth into its prey and with another single twist of its neck rips away an enormous chunk of flesh. Swallowing this in a gulp, it buries its jaws once more in the duckbill's flesh, hardly waiting to swallow one gob of meat before it is gouging out another.

Half an hour later, the tyrannosaur's great appetite is satisfied. It rises slowly. Moving lazily, it passes out of sight among the trees, in search of a comfortable sleeping place.

Most scientists think that's how Tyrannosaurus got its food—hunting and killing its prey, savagely. But *was* Tyrannosaurus really such a terrible killer? Other scientists think not. They point out that Tyrannosaurus was too big to be able to move very quickly and that most other dinosaurs probably could have outrun him. And Tyrannosaurus's tiny, two-fingered claws would not have been any use at all for grabbing and holding prey. These scientists believe that Tyrannosaurus was a carrion eater, like a vulture or a jackal, and could only live off the bodies of animals that had died.

But that seems hard to believe. For when we look at the fossil skeleton of this great beast—the enormous head with its sharp, bristling teeth and the powerful body—it's hard not to think of Tyrannosaurus as a terrible killer, truly the king of beasts not only for its own time but for all time to come.

Ankylosaurus—THE ARMORED DINOSAUR

ANKYLOSAURUS was a dinosaur that wore armor and carried a club!

Ankylosaurus means "stiff lizard," but a better name for this creature might have been "bumpy lizard!" For Ankylosaurus's head, neck, back, and tail were covered with a bumpy armor of thick, rock-hard ovals of bone embedded in tough skin. This armor was not stiff and solid like the shell of a turtle; it was flexible, like the bony shell of a modern armadillo.

But Ankylosaurus undoubtedly used its armor in the same way that a turtle does. If Ankylosaurus was attacked, all it had to do was crouch down with its legs tucked beneath itself and its soft throat and belly pressed tightly against the ground. In this position there was nothing for an attacker to bite but a mass of bony bumps. And the hungry Tyrannosaurus or other flesh eater that tried to bite through an Ankylosaurus's armor would have found itself with a mouth full of broken teeth.

However, Ankylosaurus didn't depend on its armor alone for protection. It could fight, and fight well. Its teeth were blunt and weak, and it had no sharp claws, but its tail was thick and powerful and tipped with a huge, round mass of bone—nothing

less than a massive and deadly club! When Ankylosaurus was attacked it probably waited until its tail was in striking distance of the attacker, and then—THUMP! The tail whipped around and smashed into the other dinosaur's legs or body with enough force to crack bones and send it sprawling. And the flesh eater whose leg was broken by a blow from an ankylosaur's tail was as good as dead, for it would be unable to walk and hunt and would starve to death.

Ankylosaurus wasn't one of the biggest dinosaurs. It was only a little more than 15 feet long and no more than 4 or 5 feet high. But it was built as solidly as a boulder, with a wide, bulky body and squat, solid legs like the legs of an elephant. Its feet, too, were broad and flat like an elephant's feet, and for the same reason—they had to support the weight of a heavy body.

Ankylosaurus's head was broad and blunt and looked much like the head of a horned lizard of today. This resemblance was increased by shelves of bone that stuck out above its eyes, coming to points on each side of its head. These shelves helped protect Ankylosaurus's eyes. Even its eyelids had bony shields imbedded in them!

It's easy to imagine this broad, bulky

Tyrannosau

ANKYLOSAURUS

Paleoscincus

beast crunching through the underbrush like a big armored tank, its head swinging from side to side as it peered about with its little eyes for the kind of soft plants its weak teeth could chew. Despite its bulk and armor and terrible tail, Ankylosaurus was really a harmless reptile that spent most of its time looking for food and would only fight if attacked.

There were many different kinds of these bone-armored, plant-eating dinosaurs living in all parts of the world from about 130 million to 70 million years ago. Some lived at the same time as Ankylosaurus, and some lived millions of years earlier. They all belonged to the ankylosaur family, but they all have different names. And each had its own kind of armor, and usually, its own special kind of weapon on its tail.

Paleoscincus, which means "ancient lizard," lived in North America about 80 million years ago, some 10 million years before Ankylosaurus. The two animals looked much alike and were about the same size, but Paleoscincus's armor consisted of bands of bony rectangles running down its back and tail, and rows of big, sharp spikes along its sides. Paleoscincus must have depended mostly on its armor for protection, because it doesn't seem to have had a club on its tail.

Another North American armored dinosaur was *Nodosaurus,* meaning "knobbed lizard." Its 12-foot-long body was covered with round bumps of bone. Nodosaurus was related to Paleoscincus, and like that animal, did not have a club tail either. Its tail was like a long, stiff rod of bone. It

probably couldn't have used such a tail as a weapon and depended entirely on its armor for protection.

Euoplocephalus was another North American ankylosaur. In fact, it was the ancestor of Ankylosaurus. It was only about half as long as Ankylosaurus, and its armor consisted of big, pointed knobs that stuck up all over its body. On the end of its tail was a huge ball of bone with sharp ridges on it.

Pinacosaurus was an armored dinosaur that lived in Mongolia and was related to Ankylosaurus and Euoplocephalus. Sharp spikes pointed up from its back, sides, legs, and tail. Its tail was quite a bit longer than the tails of most other armored dinosaurs and ended in a broad, flat piece of bone with sharp edges. It looked like a battle-ax, and that's probably what Pinacosaurus used it for!

Polacanthus and Acanthopholis were two kinds of armored dinosaurs that lived in what is now England and northern Europe. They were both somewhat smaller than Ankylosaurus, and their bodies were much slimmer, with longer legs, necks, and tails. Polacanthus had a double row of enormous, sharp horns running up its back to its hips. A big, curved shield of bone covered its hips, and then a double row of flat, bony points ran all the way down to the end of its tail. Acanthopholis had a whole mixture of spikes, knobs, bumps, and rectangles covering its body.

And there were other members of the ankylosaur family besides these. Fossils of nearly 30 different kinds of these bulky,

54

Acanthopholis

Polacanthus

armored beasts have been found in North and South America, Europe, and Asia. Almost all of these fossils were upside down when they were found. Because of this, many scientists think that Ankylosaurus may have lived in watery, swampy places. For, an ankylosaur that died in such a place would have sunk down and turned over onto its back from the weight of its armor.

But maybe some of these were armored dinosaurs that had been turned over—maybe they had been killed by flesh eaters! As you know, if a turtle is turned over onto its back it is helpless. And because of the weight of armor that covered its back, the same thing could have happened to an ankylosaur. Chances are that more than once an enraged and hungry tyrannosaur or Albertosaurus, clawing savagely with its back feet at an armored dinosaur's body, managed to turn the ankylosaur over onto its back so that its unprotected throat and belly were exposed. In an instant the flesh eater's teeth would have been savagely tearing into the unprotected flesh! And like a turtle on its back, all the unfortunate ankylosaur could have done in such a situation was to feebly kick its legs and probably thrash about, vainly trying to strike its enemy with its war-club tail.

Armored dinosaurs undoubtedly did become food for hungry flesh eaters from time to time, but this certainly must not have happened very often. For the most part these squat, bulky creatures must have been quite safe inside their thick shells of bony armor and well defended by their war-club tails. Ankylosaurs seem to have been quite common in prehistoric times; there were many different kinds of them, and they were around for nearly 60 million years. This seems to prove that the combination of armor and a war-club tail was pretty successful.

Struthiomimus — THE OSTRICH DINOSAUR

THE MIDDAY SUN gleams hotly on the gray-green surface of a broad, winding river. Above the water dragonflies dart and hover in search of prey. On the muddy banks a variety of creatures—frogs, turtles, snakes, and a host of insects—creep, crawl, hop, and stalk in search of food.

Moving along the riverbank is an odd, ungainly creature. It has a tiny head perched atop a long, thin neck. It strides along on two birdlike back legs, holding its smaller front legs against its chest, kangaroo fashion. A long, slender tail stretches stiffly out behind it, and its head bobs with every step it takes.

Abruptly the creature stops. It turns its head jerkily from side to side, surveying the stretch of riverbank and the nearby forest edge for a sign of danger. Satisfied that all is well, it cocks its head and peers at the ground by its feet where something has caught its attention.

Bending down, it scrabbles in the earth with its three-fingered hands. After a few moments it straightens up, holding an egg, about the size and shape of a potato, that it has dug out of the muddy earth. Curving its neck, the animal prods fiercely at the egg with its beaklike jaws. Its efforts to

break the shell are shortly rewarded, and it slurps down the egg's contents.

Dropping the empty shell, the creature cocks its head and peers again at the ground. It stoops once more, as if to resume digging. But suddenly its body whips upright. It stands frozen, with head half-turned and eyes staring unblinkingly toward the forest, some distance away.

From among the trees another creature appears. It is a much larger animal, with a heavy body and tail and powerful legs. Its massive head is split into huge jaws filled with sharp teeth. The jaws widen as it catches sight of the long-necked creature. With immense strides it moves forward.

But fast as a finger snap, the long-necked creature is running away. It moves with surprising speed, its skinny legs kicking up spurts of dirt as they churn up and down. It is soon no more than a dot in the distance, safely out of reach . . . .

That imaginary look into the past illustrates what was probably a typical adventure in the life of a most curious dinosaur that lived on the North American continent about 75 million years ago. It is called *Struthiomimus*, which means "ostrich imitator." And this gawky reptile of

Crocodiles

STRUTHIOMIMUS

Frogs   Pachyopl

long ago certainly was a remarkable "imitation" of that big, gawky bird, the ostrich, which lives today in the deserts of Africa.

Of course, no one ever saw a live Struthiomimus, but its fossil skeleton looks very much like the skeleton of a modern ostrich. They are both about the same size—8 feet tall. Both have the same kind of legs. Both have ridiculously tiny heads on top of identically long, skinny necks. And most unusual for a dinosaur, Struthiomimus had no teeth. It had a toothless bill that was almost exactly like the bill of an ostrich!

There were differences between the two creatures, of course, for Struthiomimus was a reptile and an ostrich is a bird. Struthiomimus had long, slender arms—very much like human arms—instead of wings, and a dry, leathery skin instead of feathers. And it had a long reptilian tail.

But because Struthiomimus was generally so much like an ostrich, most scientists think it probably acted much as an ostrich does. For example, we know that an ostrich can run faster than a racehorse, and since Struthiomimus had the same kind of legs, it was undoubtedly a mighty fast runner, too. Running was probably its way of protecting itself, for while an ostrich can kick hard enough to break a lion's back, and Struthiomimus's legs were equally powerful, kicking would have done the dinosaur no good. Its chief danger was from the monster, flesh-eating Tyrannosaurus and the smaller, but equally terrible Albertosaurus. Either of these creatures could have gobbled up a Struthiomimus as easily as you can eat a hot dog, and a kick wouldn't

Ostrich

"Ostrich Mimic" (Struthiomimus)

have bothered them any more than a mosquito bite.

Even though it had no teeth, Struthiomimus was probably a meat eater. Its "pecking" beak was well equipped for snapping up insects, worms, and perhaps small, soft-bodied lizards, which it gulped down whole just as ostriches do today. Possibly it could have managed to eat some of the small, ratlike mammals that lived at that time, too.

Ostriches eat plants, and some scientists think that Struthiomimus may have eaten plants, too. With its handlike claws it would have been able to pull down the lower branches of trees so that it could nip off the soft leaves, buds, and fruit. However, other scientists doubt that Struthiomimus's bill was strong enough to chop up plant material.

Although ostriches don't eat eggs, most scientists think that Struthiomimus may have done so. With the whole world full of egg-laying reptiles there were undoubtedly plenty of eggs to be found, and Struthiomimus was well able to dig eggs out of nests and hold them in its hands while it cracked them with its beaklike jaws. For that matter, there were many kinds of birds in the world when Struthiomimus was alive, so it may have occasionally feasted on some of their eggs, too.

Struthiomimus wasn't the only kind of ostrich dinosaur. It had a cousin named *Ornithomimus,* which means "bird imitator" and which looked very much like Struthiomimus. Ornithomimus lived in North America, too, but fossils of both it

58

and Struthiomimus have also been found in Asia.

These ostrich dinosaurs were a widespread and successful group of dinosaurs. Most scientists think they should have been able to survive, perhaps right into modern times. But between 70 and 65 million years ago, Struthiomimus and all its kin became extinct just as mysteriously as did all the other dinosaurs.

There are a great many questions about dinosaurs, but the biggest question of all is, Why did they become extinct? Many other kinds of animals that lived at the time of the last dinosaurs are still in the world today—snakes, lizards, crocodiles, turtles, and many kinds of insects, fish, and sea animals. But every single kind of dinosaur is gone—big ones, small ones, plant eaters, and flesh eaters. And many other kinds of animals that lived at the time of the dinosaurs became extinct at about the same time. It was as if something came along and wiped out certain kinds of animals while leaving others unharmed. What could have done such a thing? We don't know. We only know that it did happen.

So, you'll never be able to see a live dinosaur. But you may have the chance to see something very much like one. If you ever visit a zoo that has ostriches on exhibit, watch them as they move about. The way they walk and run and twist their heads about on their long, skinny necks is probably very much the way Struthiomimus did those things! Squint your eyes and use your imagination. Pretend that the ostriches have long tails and leathery skin instead of feathers. It will seem as if you are actually watching one of the strange ostrich dinosaurs that trotted about on the banks of the rivers that wound through the lowland forests of North America those many millions of years ago.

Ornithomimus

Phobosuchus

Index

PRINTED IN U.S.A.